Is
Alberto
For
Real?

**Compiled by
Sidney Hunter**

INTERNATIONAL DISTRIBUTORS

Christ The Way Publications, Inc.
P.O. Box 43120, Eastwood Square
Kitchener, Ont. N5H 6S9, Canada

B. McCall Barbour
28 George IV Bridge
Edinburgh, Scotland/UK EH1 1ES
Tel: 031-225 4816

New Zealand Evangelistic Society
P.O. Box 50096
Porirua, Wellington, New Zealand

Evangelistic Literature Enterprise
P.O. Box 5010
Brendale, Q'ld., Australia 4500
Tel: (07) 3205-7100

Gospel Publishers
P.O. Box 1
Westhoven 2142, South Africa
Tel: (11) 673-3157
Fax: (11) 673-2644

Sword Distributors
P.O. Box 3459
Parklands 2121, South Africa
Tel/Fax: (11) 486-3361

Chick's
Postfach 1166
D-51387 Burscheid
Germany
Tel. 02174/63815
Fax 02174/2799

ISBN: 0-937958-29-8 Fourth Printing
199/C
Library of Congress Catalog Card No: 88-072330

Published by Chick Publications
P.O. Box 662, Chino, CA 91708-0662 USA
Tel: (909) 987-0771 • Fax: (909) 941-8128
http://chick.com

By E-Mail: postmaster@chick.com

Printed in the United States of America

INTRODUCTION

"Is Alberto for real?"

That is a controversial question I have been asked many times by those who have read of Dr. Alberto Rivera in various Chick Publications materials.

Alberto Rivera is a former Roman Catholic Jesuit priest who was converted to Christ. Once saved he began exposing behind-the-scenes activities of the Roman Catholic church.

Chick Publications, in the United States, has produced a series of Crusaders comics, ALBERTO, DOUBLE CROSS, THE GODFATHERS, THE FORCE and THE FOUR HORSEMEN, which include portions of the life story of Alberto Rivera, and other volatile information that he gave them.

The comics have had a varied effect on those who have read them. Some have become extremely hostile, while many others have had their eyes opened and been converted to Christ.

Alberto's testimony has been challenged in most cases by those who hold an ecumenical or pro-Roman Catholic position. Roman Catholics, obviously, are the most upset by Alberto's shocking statements. Some have attacked, either the person of Alberto Rivera, in an effort to discredit him; or the information he has given, alleging it to be extreme or even fraudulent.

Catholics who know the facts of their church seldom attempt to refute what Alberto says about the Catholic church. Therefore, their attacks against him come primarily in the form of relentless character assassinations.

In preparing an answer to one of Dr. Rivera's critics, Rev. Fred J. Buick and Helmut Silbach of the Perth Free Presbyterian Church have done a vast amount of research which enables us to give well-documented answers to the questions that will be answered in this book.

My role has been to compile all this information in book form to answer many of the questions asked about Dr. Rivera's claims. It is our prayer that God will use our efforts to accomplish two things:

1. Convince you that Alberto Rivera was in

fact what he says he was, and:

2. Enable you to give clear and factual answers to those who question the validity of Dr. Rivera's testimony.

Though many have tried over the last 10 years, none has successfully refuted the claims that Dr. Rivera has made against the Roman Catholic church.

The purpose of this book is to refute the most frequently made charges against the content of the above mentioned books and against Dr. Rivera personally.

Sid Hunter
Strathpine, Q'ld., Australia

PUBLISHERS FOREWORD

Here at Chick Publications, we frequently receive reports of well known "Christian" leaders who attack us because of our stand on Roman Catholicism. They continually repeat the well-worn Catholic position on Alberto Rivera, doing everything they can to discredit him, yet ignoring the facts entirely.

Several years ago, when Dr. Rivera first told me his amazing story, he showed me a tremendous amount of documents, letters, I.D. cards and photographs of himself as a priest, wearing his vestments. All this information gave me absolute proof that he had in fact been a Jesuit priest.

Dr. Rivera warned me that the forces of Rome would attack me without mercy if I dared to write his story. He said they would do their best to destroy our reputation by flooding the country with false information.

I prayed about it, and the Lord gave me the go-ahead to print his story. I felt it was vital to get Dr. Rivera's message both to the body of believers who use our materials, and to the multiplied millions of unsaved Roman Catholics who are being deceived by this false religious system.

I was totally committed even unto death to obey the Lord and expose this whore of the book of Revelation.

I am shocked by those who claim to be experts on all the other enemies of the gospel, yet never open their mouths about the spiritual whoredom of Rome. I can only repeat the warning of the Apostle Paul, the writer of the book of Romans, that great epistle on the doctrine of salvation by faith, (not works, penance, or being religious):

> "Now I beseech you, brethren, mark them which cause division and offences **contrary to the doctrine which ye have learned**; and avoid them. For they that are such serve not our Lord Jesus Christ, but their own belly; and by good words and fair speeches deceive the hearts of the simple."
>
> Romans 16:17-18

After personally knowing Dr. Rivera and closely watching both his life and his vibrant soul-winning ministry for the last ten years, I am totally convinced that he is a true servant of God.

I've seen the physical attacks on both him and

his wife. I've seen the bullet holes in their home. I've seen him ruthlessly slandered by Catholic-controlled "Christian" magazines.

The more he's persecuted, the more convinced I am that his message is true and vitally important. I rejoice that because of his willingness to expose Rome, many precious Roman Catholics have been saved and now know the Lord Jesus Christ as their personal Savior. They have left the "mother of harlots," and are now serving God in truth, according to His blessed Word.

I know I will stand before the Lord some day and learn of the multitudes who escaped the burning flames of hell. They will spend eternity basking in the warm glow of heaven because they learned the blessed truth through Dr. Rivera's story.

On that day I know I'll look back and recall the high cost of exposing Rome but conclude that all the attacks and persecutions were worth it. I know my only thought will be, "Praise God for the precious souls that were won to Christ."

Without question, Dr. Rivera is for real:

* The fact that no one has ever disproved his priestly credentials proves he's real.

* The persecution he's endured since he began exposing Rome proves he's real.

* The thousands of souls that have been saved through his ministry prove he's real.

* History, and the writings of many others prove he's real.

All the facts prove one thing: Alberto Rivera is for real. And the message he tells is just as real. It is not a message of hate, as the Catholic hierarchy likes to insist. Rather, it is the ultimate message of love . . . to willingly suffer the attacks and persecution to awaken people to the false teachings of this corrupt religious system.

May the eyes of many precious Roman Catholics be opened and may their souls be won to Christ through the information contained in this short book.

That is our prayer and our goal.

Your brother in Christ,

Jack

Jack T. Chick

Table of Contents

Chapter 1

12 Most Frequently Heard Charges Against Alberto Answered

In this chapter, we will face head-on the 12 most frequently heard charges against Alberto Rivera. Our approach will be to write out each charge one at a time and then follow it with our answer.

Please note that our answers shall be totally independent of any material or sources which originated from Rivera or Chick Publications.

Charge No. 1:

It is extreme to claim that the Jesuits infiltrate Protestant and other churches.

Answer: Why should it be considered extreme to claim that Roman Catholic Jesuits would infiltrate Protestant and other churches? Does

11

not the Bible warn us that we must watch out for infiltrators who will creep into the true church of Jesus Christ "not sparing the flock?"

> "For I know this, that after my departing shall grievous wolves enter in among you, not sparing the flock." Acts 20:29

> "For there are certain men crept in unawares, who were before of old ordained to this condemnation . . ." Jude 4

Nino Lo Bello, in his book, **The Vatican Papers** – published by New English Library 1982, in the 19th chapter entitled, "The Vatican's Spy Network," makes it very clear that the Vatican has the most efficient and widespread spy network in the whole world. It outclasses even the Russian KGB. He states that this group of espionage agents came to be known by the popes as Sodalitium Pianum, and it includes every priest, nun and monk anywhere on earth.

He calculates the Pope's spy network to be in the region of 1.605 million persons consisting of diocesan priests, regular priests, seminarians, religious males and nuns, and that indeed, there are many full-time trained agents.

Now what do agents do but infiltrate other organizations, and what organizations would

Catholic spies infiltrate if not other churches, especially true churches of Jesus Christ?

Permit me to quote a passage from the reliable old Protestant classic, **The History Of Protestanism** by Rev. J. A. Wylie, page 412, Vol. II:

"There was no disguise they (the Jesuits) could not assume, and therefore, there was no place into which they could not penetrate. They could enter unheard the closet of the Monarch, or the Cabinet of the Statesman. They could sit unseen in convocation or General Assembly, and mingle unsuspected in the deliberations and debates.

"There was no tongue they could not speak, and no creed they could not profess, and thus there was no people among whom they might not sojourn, and no church whose membership they might not enter and whose functions they might not discharge. They could execrate the Pope with the Lutheran, and swear the Solemn League with the Covenanter."

Alberto is by no means the only person suggesting that Roman Catholic spies infiltrate other churches. Anyone who has read any reputable history books must come to the same conclusion.

Somewhere along the line we've swallowed the lie that Christians can peacefully co-exist with a Satanic religious system that is leading multiplied millions of souls to hell. Satan will not have it so! He constantly seeks to infiltrate his enemies that he may bring about their destruction.

Charge No. 2:

Rivera is wrong in saying that St. Ignatius of Loyola was the founder of the Jesuits.

Answer: The **Encyclopedia Britannica** Vol. XIII, page 1011, says that the **Society Of Jesus** is "a Roman Catholic order of clerks regular, founded by St. Ignatius of Loyola in 1540."

The same document refers to the Jesuit order as being "a principal agent of the Counter-Reformation" (1973 edition). The Britannica also tells us in Vol. XI, page 1096 that the Illuminati was "organized along Jesuit lines."

So then, this is not the wild notion of one man. It is undeniable history, available to anyone who chooses to pick up an Encyclopedia Britannica. If you are going to accuse Alberto of lying, you must make the same charge of the Encyclopedia

Britannica. Why would the Encyclopedia Britannica lie about this? The simple fact is, they wouldn't. Both they and Rivera are telling the truth. And a great many people know it.

The difference between Alberto and most others is this:

>   1. He was on the inside of Rome's religious system and knows the facts personally.
>
>   2. He is willing to suffer the consequences for speaking out boldly about the powerful whore of Revelation.

The results of such actions are not a mystery to those who genuinely know God:

> "Yea, and all that will live godly in Christ Jesus **shall suffer persecution**." II Timothy 3:12

But the suffering is well worth it when combined with this heavenly promise:

> "Blessed are ye, when men shall hate you, and when they shall separate you from their company, and shall reproach you, and cast out your name as evil, for the Son of man's sake." Luke 6:22

CHARGE NO. 3

Rivera's "Conspiracy Theory" is extreme and paranoid.

Answer: There are only two ways in which world history can be explained:

1. The accidental theory. All events, such as those world depressions, revolutions, wars and political plots are the results of pure chance. Such a view is as ridiculous as belief in evolution!

2. The conspiratorial theory. World events such as mentioned above, take place because some influential people want them to happen and make them happen. People with power meet behind closed doors and work out plans to achieve their aims. The most precise way to describe such conduct is – conspiracy.

To us, the conspiratorial theory makes far more sense than the accidental theory. The conspiracy claims Rivera has made are by no means extreme and paranoid. Indeed, many respected and thorough researchers have, after many years of painstaking research, come to the conclusion that there is a conspiracy at work which desires to control the world by controlling the banks, commerce and the media.

And I need not mention to students of the Bible,

the accidental theory contradicts the entire theme of the Bible, not to mention large portions of Bible prophecy.

I give you here the titles of eleven books in which the authors, who are also listed, make their conspiracy beliefs known.

1. **None Dare Call It Conspiracy** – Gary Allen
2. **The Rockefeller File** – Gary Allen
3. **Proofs Of A Conspiracy** – John Robinson A.M.
4. **Descent Into Slavery** – Des Griffin
5. **Fourth Reich Of The Rich** – Des Griffin
6. **The Red Fog Over America** – W. G. Carr
7. **The New Unhappy Lords** – A. K. Chesterton
8. **National Suicide** – Anthony C. Sutton
9. **Betrayal By Rulers** – Michael Sturdza
10. **The Naked Capitalist** – W. Cleon Skousen
11. **Series of tapes by Dr. Stuart Crane**, made in Montreal in 1976.

While we do not agree with all that these men have written, nevertheless, the one common fact on which they all seem to agree is that there is a conspiracy at work in the world. These conspirators, they conclude, are attempting to manipulate and rule the world through their control of the banks, commerce and media. So, in that respect, they agree with Rivera's claims.

The one area where Rivera differs from them is the powers behind the scenes. The other authors basically blame the Illuminati, the International Bankers or the Zionists. These smaller groups form only a part of this conspiracy by evil forces.

Rivera, on the other hand, takes a more Biblical stance and blames Mystery Babylon, the city on seven hills (i.e., Romanism) as understood by the great Protestant Reformers. (See Rev. 17, 18.)

Surely then, Rivera is not alone in his view, but rather is just one among an almost endless line of respected authors, including modern writers, who are saying much the same thing.

Read the following books by Avro Manhattan:

- * **Catholic Power Today**
- * **Catholic Terror Today**
- * **The Vatican Moscow Washington Alliance**

* **The Vatican Billions**
* **Vietnam, Why Did We Go?**

Other good books include:

* **The Vatican Against Europe**,
  by Edmond Paris
* **The Secret History Of The Jesuits**, by Edmond Paris.
* **Peter's Tomb Recently Discovered**, by F. P. Peterson.
* **The Broadcasting Controversy – The Pope And Catholic Action**, by O. T. Beswick B. Sc.
* **Fifty Years In The "Church" Of Rome**, by Charles Chiniquy.
* **What About The Silent Conspiracy?** by Andrew Sinclair

For more information see also the book **No Pope Here**, by Dr. Ian Paisley. Or get a copy of his cassette tape **The Black Pope and His Murder Men**.

And this list is by no means complete. We could recommend many more books. These writers are saying more or less the same thing as Rivera, that

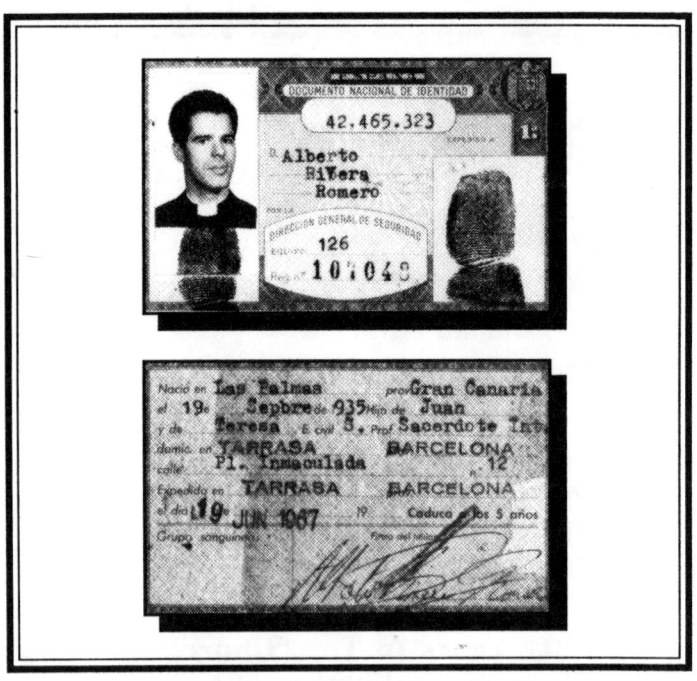

The identification card above was issued by the Spanish government in Spain in 1967, under the rule of the dictator, Franco. His security forces were equally as strict as the Gestapo in Germany.

Alberto had to supply his birth certificate, identification papers and positive proof from his archdiocese that he was a priest. He had to be approved by several security organizations similar to our C. I. A. and F. B. I., to receive this document. There is no way it could be a forgery. This is positive proof that Alberto was a priest.

the Vatican is the chief conspirator.

One more thing. The fact that the Jesuits united with the Illuminati has, to some extent, been recognized by the late W. G. Carr in his book **The Red Fog Over America**. Based on facts, backed up with personal experiences, he contends on pages 225-227 that the Illuminati was actually **inside** the Vatican.

Now, that is not so far from what Rivera is saying, is it? Rivera is certainly not alone in what he is saying. To call the man extreme and paranoid is, to put it frankly, grossly unfair and false.

Charge No. 4:

Dr. Rivera's claim that Ignatius of Loyola founded the Illuminati is paranoid.

Answer: Without going deeply into this claim, we can prove it is not farfetched at all. First, it is an unshakeable fact that the founder of the modern Bavarian Illuminati was a trained Jesuit named Adam Weishaupt from Ingolstadt, Bavaria. Weishaupt was a professor at Ingolstadt University, which was the center of the Jesuit Counter-Reformation. (See Encyclopedia Britannica Vol. XII, p. 251.)

Ingolstadt was the center where the Jesuits were flourishing in 1556. (See **History Of Protestantism** by Wylie, Vol. II, page 413.) Can we really believe that Weishaupt would have been allowed to continue his professorship in a Jesuit controlled University if he had deserted them? No way! All evidence suggests that he continued to work for the Jesuits, establishing the order of the Illuminati for them.

Whatever the case, Rivera's claim that Ignatius of Loyola founded the Illuminati is by no means paranoid. Especially not when the fact is taken into account that Loyola was tried before a court in 1527 for sympathizing with the Alumbrados (i.e. the Spanish Illuminati). Here is what the Encyclopedia Britannica has to say on this issue:

> "The Alumbrados came especially from among the reformed Franciscans and Jesuits, and St. Ignatius Loyola was charged in 1527 with sympathizing with them."   Vol. 1, page 693

So, the Spanish Illuminati drew most of its recruits from Roman Catholic sources, the Franciscans and Jesuits, and Loyola was charged with being in favor with them.

The persecution that Rivera has suffered for making such claims is nothing new. God's prophets down through the ages have endured similar treatment for exposing false religious teachings. However, the Bible promises Rivera a special blessing in heaven because none of the evil accusations that have been spoken against him have ever been proven true:

> "Blessed are ye, when men shall revile you, and persecute you, and shall say all manner of evil against you falsely, for my sake. Rejoice, and be exceeding glad: for great is your reward in heaven: for so persecuted they the prophets which were before you."
>
> Matthew 5: 11-12

If Alberto's claims are wrong, then prove him wrong with cold, hard facts, not with cheap personal character attacks against him.

Charge No. 5:

Rivera is wrong to claim the Roman Catholic system tried to annihilate the Jews.

Answer: This is a plain fact of history. During the Council of Latern held in AD 1215, all "heretics" – Jews and Protestants – were condemned to death. This decree, as far as I am aware, has never been repealed. In chapter XIII

of **Fifty Years In The "Church" Of Rome** by
Chiniquy, published by Chick Publications, you
will read the following two quotes on page 56:

> "Roman Catholics have not only the
> right, but it is their duty, to kill here-
> tics."

> "We excommunicate and anathematize
> every heresy that exalts itself against
> the holy and orthodox Catholic faith,
> condemning all heretics, by whatever
> name they may be known, for though
> their faces differ, they are tied together
> by their tails. Such as are condemned
> are to be delivered over to the existing
> secular powers to receive due punish-
> ment."

It is an undeniable fact of history that the Jews
have suffered persecution at the hands of Popery
for centuries. Rivera is completely right when
he makes this claim.

The German author, Otto Markmann, in his book,
Irrtumer Der Katholischen Kirche, says:

> "Crusades – During the cruel crusades,
> which the popes instigated, we remem-
> ber atrocities committed by the Mercen-
> aries, the capture of Constantinople and
> the setting up of the Latin Patriarchate

in the East. During the first crusade, which was called by Pope Alexander II in the year 1063, the north Spanish city of Barbestro was conquered. Fifty thousand Moslems were tortured and slaughtered.

"In Constantinople the most horrific Jewish pogroms were conducted. Jews were burned alive in the Synagogues. The second crusade of 1147 started just as the first, with murdering Jews and the slaughter of Moslems in Portugal."

In 1377, Jews were slaughtered in the Bavarian village of Deggendorf. Ferrabd Martinez, who was Archbishop coadjutor in Seville, conducted the baptizing war in Seville with the cry, "Be baptized or die." He destroyed the Jewish community of 30,000 members. Four thousand were murdered and the rest were sold as slaves. Ten thousand of the persecuted Jews, in fear of death, submitted to the forceful conversions. They became known as the "Marannen."

The book **Irrtumer Der Katholischen Kirche** also supports what Alberto is saying:

"The horrors went through all of Aragon, Kastilien, Barcelona, Valencia, and Mallorca. The holy Vicente called during this 'holy war' for a holy hate –

it remains until this twentieth century. Under the guidance of the great inquisitor, Thomas of Torquemada, they burned during the inquisition, in three days in Toledo, 2,400 Marannen.

"In the year 1506, the monks of Lissabon celebrated the 'blood wedding' and burned during Easter on two days, over two thousand Jews. What a great sin of the Roman Catholic church against the chosen nation."

Let us now proceed to the great book by Avro Manhattan entitled **The Vatican Moscow Washington Alliance.** On pages 219-220, he writes:

"It is important, although it may be difficult for some to recognize the religious nature of the Communist/Zionist/Catholic political configuration. Although deliberately muted in public pronouncements, behind the Zionist banner there was to be found the ancient Messianic hope for the coming of a global theocracy, as predicted by all the seers and prophets of Zion. It was to be a theocracy in which Jehovah, not Christ, was to be King.

"The spectre of the creation of such a theocracy has haunted the inner cham-

26

bers of the Catholic church from her earliest inception, and still is a dominant fear.

"In Vatican eyes, therefore, the millenarian yearning for a global Hebrew theocracy, represents a deadly threat to the eschatological teachings of the Catholic church. When translated into concrete political terms, such a view spells not only rivalry, but implacable enmity."

Furthermore, we turn to a recent newspaper article which adds great credibility to Rivera's claims. On page 75 of the Dec. 4, 1985 issue of Perth's **West Australian** newspaper, a paper most definitely not accused of anti-Catholic bias, an article appeared entitled, **Prelate: Too Soon To Ask Forgiveness**. Dateline: Rome, Tevs:

The article said in part:

"It would be premature for the Catholic church to ask the forgiveness of the Jews for centuries of persecution, a Vatican Cardinal said yesterday. A group of Italians recently signed a petition requesting the Synod of Bishops to issue a statement seeking Jewish forgiveness."

Although it has been forty years since the last

of the Jews were tortured and butchered in concentration camps by leaders of the so-called "holy mother church," this paper admits it is still too soon for the Catholic church to expect forgiveness for their heinous crimes!

I now refer to Andrew Sinclair's book **The Great Silence Conspiracy**. On page 8, he quotes from the **Encyclopedia Britannica**, 11th Edition, Vol. II, page 37:

> "The Roman Catholic church has always been, of course, the font of anti-Semitism. Anti-Semitism was almost unknown in Tzarist Greek Catholic Russia until after the partitions of Poland in 1772 and 1795. Russian anti-Semitism was imbibed from Roman Catholic Poland. The Spanish 'Holy Inquisition' was founded to destroy the Jews in Spain."

Need we quote further than this to show the thinker that what Rivera and Chick are saying today is vastly verified by writers of past ages?

Charge No. 6:

Dr. Rivera is wrong in associating the Jesuits with the setting up of World War I.

Answer: The following statement is made on page 63 of F. Paul Peterson's book **Peter's Tomb Recently Discovered**:

"The Popes have been in, or instigated most, if not all of the European wars down through the centuries."

In the book, **The Vatican Against Europe**, by Edmond Paris, we read:

"Pope Pius X in his hatred against orthodox Christians, was continually inciting Emperor Francis Joseph of Austria – Hungary to 'chastize the Serbians.' After Sarajevo, on 26th July, 1914, Baron Ritter, Bavarian representative of the Holy See, wrote to his Government: 'The Pope approves of Austria's harsh treatment of Serbia. He has no great opinion of the armies of Russia and France in the event of a war against Germany. The Cardinal secretary of State does not see when Austria could make war if she does not decide to do so now . . .'

"There in the true colours is the Vicar of Christ, the gentle apostle of peace, the holy Pontiff whom pious authors represent as having died of sorrow at seeing the outbreak of war."

Again from the same book, page 47:

"Thus it is proved that Pius X and his
Secretary of State, when they encour-
aged the most Catholic Emperor to make
war, were coldly contemplating the con-
sequences of their act: a general conflict
which would set the Central European
Empires against France and Russia.

"They believed they had accurately es-
timated the strength of the different
forces involved. But what his holiness
and his accomplice had not forseen was
the participation in the war of England,
and finally of the entire Anglo-Saxon
world, a participation which was to
thwart their plans, tip the scales in
favor of France and liberate the orthodox populations from the Viennese yoke.

"Hence the responsibility for the crime
is beyond doubt an enormous crime
which, over a period of four years, was
to throw into the charnel-house millions
of Christian corpses, all the flower of
European youth, and a crime all the
more odious for being completely pre-
meditated.

"One may say quite specifically that in
1914 the Roman church started the

hellish series of wars. It was then that the tribute of blood, which she has always taken from the peoples, began to swell to a veritable torrent."

The above book, and others, are full of evidence that proves the veracity of statements made by Alberto Rivera. The more recent publication, **The Secret History Of The Jesuits**, by Edmond Paris, also mentions similar facts.

In the book, **Fifty Years In The "Church" Of Rome**, by Charles Chiniquy, published by Chick Publications, Inc., we read similar facts. On page 296, we find that Abraham Lincoln agrees with Alberto Rivera. Mr. Lincoln said:

"This war (the American Civil War) would never have been possible without the sinister influence of the Jesuits. We owe it to Popery that we now see our land reddened with the blood of her noblest sons. Though there were great differences of opinion, between the South and the North, on the question of slavery, neither Jeff Davis nor any one of the leading men of the Confederacy would have dared to attack the North had they not relied on the promises of the Jesuits that, under the mask of democracy, the money and the arms of the Roman Catholics, even the arms of France, were at their disposal if they would attack us."

History itself bears testimony to the fact that Rome has the blood of innocent multitudes dripping from her sinister hands. Rivera is right. The Jesuits were behind World War I, just as he claims.

Charge No. 7:

Dr. Rivera is wrong in his claim that Jesuits prepared the Russian Revolution and helped Marx, Engels, Trotsky, Lenin and Stalin bring in Communism in order to destroy the Orthodox Church.

Answer: We cannot deny that the Russian Revolution was set up by outside interests. No movement of the people on its own will succeed against a modern army without outside help. The old days of Robin Hood, when a few rebels could trouble a properly trained army, are over.

Today, any rebel force that wants to be successful must have many modern weapons. How to get them is the problem. They cannot manufacture weapons themselves; nor is it possible to capture sufficient quantities of them from the enemy.

Modern examples of this are Vietnam and Af-

Below are some of the last photographs of Dr. Rivera while he was the Director of the Parish School in San Lorenzo, Tarrasa, Spain.

ghanistan. The communists in Vietnam only succeeded because of massive Russian armament shipments into North Vietnam harbors. The anti-communist forces in Afghanistan cannot succeed without limited outside help.

So it was in 1917. Without outside help, the Communist Revolution would have fizzled out quickly. **Wall Street And The Bolshevik Revolution**, the well-documented book by Anthony Sutton, shows how money was moved from German and American banks through Swedish banks into Russia for the Bolsheviks' use.

Now, the question arises, who were the powers with enough interest in the Communist movement who could send large amounts of money and enough arms to help them to victory? See **National Suicide**, by A. Sutton, page 76! The general explanation is that the German government wanted to help the Bolsheviks into power so they would end the war.

Much can be said on this point, but time does not permit. Rivera's claims as to the secret force behind the Bolshevik movement, which makes more sense than most of the others, are confirmed by Avro Manhattan in his book, **The Vatican Billions.** On pages 124-125 he writes this:

> "The overthrow of the Czarist system therefore, brought with it the inevitable

34

overthrow of the established Orthodox Church. To the Vatican, which had waged war against the Orthodox Church since the eleventh century, the downfall of her millenarian rival was too good to be true. The evil of Bolshevism could in this manner be accepted in view of its having destroyed the Orthodox Church–with one proviso, however, that it should give the Catholic church a free hand to finish the task of eliminating Orthodoxy in Russia once and for all.

"The deal was accepted, and so it came to pass that while the Vatican was fulminating against Bolshevism, the Bolsheviks in the Kremlin and the Vatican's diplomats in Rome began secret negotiations. Lenin agreed with the Pope. Machineries were set up. Papal Commissions, some headed by American prelates, were despatched to Bolshevik Russia, disguised as famine relief missions and the like.

"In Rome and elsewhere, Catholic priests were given accelerated instruction in Russian Orthodox theology and ritual. Grandiose schemes were blueprinted for taking over the Orthodox Church, lock, stock and barrel, including the claims for her former wealth and

lands; these to be put forward at a later
stage, once Catholicism had taken over."

The reason the deal fell through can be attributed
to the cleverness of Lenin, who eventually saw
through the real motives of the Vatican. Now,
if you care to read carefully the whole chapter
of the above mentioned books and **Wall Street
And The Bolshevik Revolution,** you will see
a picture emerging which is comfortably close to
the claims made by Rivera; that the Jesuits **did**
set up the Russian Revolution.

Charge No. 8:

**It is wrong to say that Jesuits wrote Hitler's
Mein Kampf as part of their master plan for
Hitler to take over Germany.**

Answer: Rivera is certainly not alone in this
belief. Andrew Sinclair says on page 9 of his book,
The Great Silence Conspiracy:

"Who wrote **Mein Kampf**? **Mein
Kampf**, the Nazi bible, was supposed to
be written by Hitler, but Otto Strasser
says in **Hitler And I** that **Mein Kampf**
was written by a Roman Catholic priest,
Father Bernhardt Stempfle, from notes

supplied by Hitler. Otto Strasser, a Roman Catholic, was one of the founders of the Nazi Party; Stempfle, a notorious anti-Semite, was a member of the Roman Catholic Order of Saint Jerome."

We find the same teaching in **The Secret History Of The Jesuits**, by Edmond Paris. On page 138, we read the following:

"The Fuhrer had come to power, thanks to the votes of the Catholic Zentrum, only five years before, but most of the objectives cynically revealed in **Mein Kampf** were already realized; this book, an insolent challenge to the western democracies, was written by the Jesuit Father Stempfle and signed by Hitler. For, as so many ignore the fact, it was the Society of Jesus which perfected the famous Pan-German programme as laid out in this book and the Fuhrer endorsed it."

Here, from the pen of two reliable outside sources of information, we have the exact same claim that Rivera is making. Once again, this is not the wild claim of one man, it is common history, available to anyone who wishes to study and find out.

Charge No. 9:

It is wrong to infer that the Jesuits started a new inquisition and continued their efforts to annihilate the Jews by bringing Mussolini, Hitler and Franco into power.

Answer: On page 15 of **The Vatican Against Europe**, by Edmond Paris, we read:

> "In 1922 Pope Pius XI donned the tiara. The Papacy had lost the first war; it was about to prepare for the second. What was happening in Europe between the two massacres? In Italy, secret negotiations took place between Papal agents and Mussolini, 'the man of providence.' The priest, Don Sturzo, chief of the Catholic Group, had full rights voted to the Duce on November, 1922. Then came the Lateran Treaty, to seal the union of Fascism and the Papacy, the conquest of Ethiopia – blessed by the clergy – and, on Good Friday 1939, the aggression against Albania.
>
> "In Germany, the Papal Nuncio in Berlin, Mgr. Pacelli and Franz von Papen, privy Chamberlain to the Pope, advocated a 'union with Rome' and concentrated on the overthrow of the Weimar Republic. The German Catho-

lics were hostile to Nazism, but were informed that the Pope himself was 'favourably disposed towards Hitler.' Consequently the Catholic Zentrum, axis of all Parliamentary majorities, voted full rights to Hitler on January 30, 1933.

"This operation was promptly followed, as in Italy, by the concluding of a Concordat which was most advantageous to the Roman church. The German Episcopate swore allegiance to the Fuhrer and Catholic Youth organizations combined with those of the Nazis ... In Spain, the Virgin appeared here and there, and effigies of Christ shed tears. These were unmistakable signs the Republic and its impious regime would not last long.

"On 31st March, 1934, the Pact of Rome was signed and pledged support of Mussolini and Hitler for the rebellion. The 'holy war' broke out. In 1937, in the midst of war, the Vatican gave dejure recognition to the government of Franco, its sword-bearer, who was later to be decorated with the Supreme Order of Christ. 'Blessed be the guns if the gospel flowers in their wake!' Soon the Catholic Action was to spread its tyranny across the ruined country. Pax Christi!"

On page 96 of the same book we read a statement by Franz von Papen, the Apostolic Nuncio – that is to say, the secular arm of Pope Pius XI. Under the heading, "Catholics and Christian Socialists Vote for Hitler's Dictatorship," von Papen writes:

"On the evening of January 30, 1933, the day when the Cabinet was constituted, I was standing behind Hitler on the balcony of the new Chancellery. We were watching an endless procession, hundreds of thousands of men who, torch in hand, were marching past Hindenburg and the Fuhrer. Hitler's face was ecstatic and when he turned to speak to me, there was a sob in his voice. 'What a tremendous task we have set ourselves, Herr von Papen!.'

"I was happy to be able to concur . . . 'You are a soldier, Herr von Papen' he said to me, 'so you know that one has always to march with the largest and strongest battalions. If you and I march together, we are assured of a majority and consequently of success!' "

Yes, indeed, Hitler marched with the strongest battalions; he marched as a Romanist in a Roman Catholic army! Much more valuable material could be gleaned from Paris' books, but let us turn to another author who will verify Rivera.

40

Now we look at **Peter's Tomb Recently Discovered In Jerusalem**, by F. Paul Peterson. In his fourth edition, 1971, page 63, we are told:

> "But some will say that Catholicism believes in God. How can they really believe in God and murder 69 million people and continue to murder Christians to this very day in Mexico, Colombia and Spain?
>
> "Even Hitler was a Catholic as were all his generals and advisers. Did the Pope ever excommunicate Hitler or any of his generals for these crimes? Never! In fact, as I have written in my book, **The Rise And Fall Of The Roman Catholic Church**, the Pope was just as much in the Second World War as was Hitler and Catholic Mussolini and therefore just as guilty of the murder of six million Jews. In fact, Popes have been in or instigated most, if not all, the European wars down through the centuries."

Let us look again at **The Vatican Moscow Washington Alliance** by Avro Manhattan. From the chapter, "The Swastika and the Triple Tiara," we learn:

> "In 1929, the Fascist government of Italy and the Vatican signed the Lateran

41

Agreement and Mussolini granted the church the extraordinary privileges it had asked. All Italian bishops were required to take an oath of allegiance to Il Duce (article 20 of the Concordat). The church had turned its back on socialism, whether of a Marxist or ostensibly Catholic kind, siding with anticommunist political forces of Europe.

"The most vigorous and powerful of these was Nazism. The Vatican helped Hitler to gain power and then helped him consolidate his grip on Germany. This was done in party by 'advising' the Catholic Party of Germany to vote for Nazi candidates.

"The Catholic vote gave Hitler the majority he needed to legally form a government in 1933. Further to this, the Vatican ordered Catholic members of the Reichstag Parliament to support legislation giving Hitler the power to rule by decree. This measure gave Hitler the dictatorial power he needed to destroy the German Communists.

"After the law had been passed, the Vatican ordered the German Catholic Party to disband, as it had previously commanded its Italian counterpart to do back in 1927. In response to the Vatican directive, the German Catholic Party demobilized in the summer of 1933.

"The whole Vatican-Hitler bargain had been conducted in secret before Hitler became Chancellor of Germany in January 1933. In June of the same year, Hitler and the Vatican signed a Concordat, under terms of which the church swore allegiance to the Nazi regime. Here are the textual words: 'I swear and promise to honour the legally constituted i.e., Nazi Government. I will endeavour to avoid all detrimental acts which might endanger it' (Article 16 of the Concordat).

" 'Soon afterward, Catholic Franz von Papen, the second in command to Hitler, put the essence of the Hitler-Vatican alliance very succinctly in these words: 'The Third Reich,' he said, 'is the first power which not only recognizes, but puts into practice, the high principles of the Papacy' (**Der Volkischer Beobachter**, Jan., 1934)."

Permit me now to prove from **The Great Silence Conspiracy**, by Andrew Sinclair that both Rivera and Chick are right on course in what they are saying.

Page 7 of that booklet asks: "Was Hitler a Roman Catholic?" Hitler, an Austrian, not a German, was the product of a Roman Catholic "education"; his parents were so closely related that an episcopal dispensation was necessary for the marriage. He was born at the Hotel Zum Pommer in Braunau, Austria, on April 20, 1889. He was born, baptized and brought up a Roman Catholic.

Dr. Henry Picker, author of **The Hitler Phenomenon**, English translation, published in 1974, joined the inner circle of Hitler's intimates in 1942. Page 8 of Picker's book says:

> Hitler "never left the church, always paid his church-rate punctually...Ever since his time as a choir boy at the Convent of Lambach, he had admired the Roman church with its organization, its ceremonies, its symbols and its banners and he copied these for his temporal ministry down to the smallest details."

Another interesting question is raised and answered on page 8 of **The Hitler Phenomenon:**

> "Where was the Nazi Party founded? It was founded in *Roman Catholic* Bavaria (emphasis theirs), Germany's Eire; its headquarters were in Munich, the Dublin of Germany."

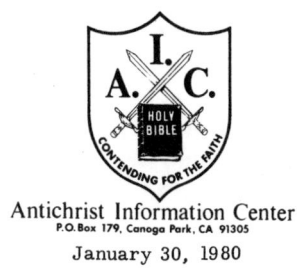

Antichrist Information Center
P.O. Box 179, Canoga Park, CA 91305

January 30, 1980

To Whom it May Concern:

I have been requested to make a statement concerning the
validity of the account of my life story in the book, "Alberto,"
published by Chick Publications, Inc.

"Alberto" is a true and actual account, and I will face a court
ot law to prove the events actually took place. I hereby challenge anyone who would refute or try to prove the facts and
information in this book are untrue. I will defend every statement made regardless of the embarrassment it may cause any
person or church.

Sincerely,

Alberto M. B. Rivera, D. Th.

45

Now go back to Sinclair's booklet, page 10:

> "When Hitler became Chancellor, who
> was his Deputy Chancellor? Baron Kon-
> stantin von Neurath, a Roman Catholic,
> was Hitler's first Foreign Minister."

Flip over one page to page 11 and you will read:

> "Who was the Nazi chief propagandist?
> The No. 1 liar of the Nazi Party, the Nazi
> Minister of Propaganda, head over
> press, radio, theatre, etc., was Dr. P. J.
> Goebbels, also a Roman Catholic.
> Konstantin, Duke of Bavaria, a Roman
> Catholic, said in his book, **The Pope**,
> page 77 that Goebbels 'received a Jesuit
> education, attended an academy in
> Catholic Rhineland, and received the
> scholarship for his training from a
> Catholic institution.' "

Sinclair goes on to say:

> "Goebbels was trained by the world's
> most brazen liars."

We quote again from page 15 of the same source:

> "Was Bormann a Roman Catholic? The
> play, THE VICAR, by Rolf Huchhuth, is
> not fiction; it is as accurate historically

as any history book. In the U.S. edition of the play, Huchhuth gives 66 pages of documentation. It has long been known that Goebbels studied for the priest-hood. The Austrian Fascist, Dollfuss, also studied for the priesthood. But Rolf Huchhuth says, "Hitler, Goebbels, Bormann, Kaltenbrunner, Hoess ... studied for the priest-hood."

So Rivera was not wrong in his claims. He was telling the plain truth, as many reputable sources verify. We must admit, though, we can certainly understand why the Roman Catholic institution is so upset that he is bringing to light these particular facts of history.

Charge No. 10:

It is wrong to say that death camps were run by Roman Catholic priests and monks and that they followed the policy of the Inquisition to examine heretics.

Answer:

"Hitler himself often stated that his mentor in anti-Semitism was the Roman Catholic chief lay conductor of political Roman Catholicism in Austria, Dr. Karl

Lueger, burgermaster of Vienna and leader of the Christian Social Party."

Again from **The Hitler Phenomenon,** page 11:

"Who were the principal Nazi murderers? Himmler, head of the Gestapo; Heydrich, his right-hand man; Kaltenbrunner, who succeeded Heydrich; Mueller and Frank, all Roman Catholics by birth and upbringing.

"Hoess, the Commandant of the infamous Auschwitz, was also a Roman Catholic. The first concentration camp was set up by Himmler at Dachau, Munich.

"Heinrich Himmler had an uncle who was a Jesuit priest. This Jesuit – Himmler director? – was arrested at the end of the war but he was not tried. He was found dead one morning in his cell. Himmler, like Goering, cheated the gallows by suicide, or so it was believed."

Charles Wighton, author of Heydrich's biography, **Heydrich**, writes on page 26 that:

"Contrary to the widely held belief that Heydrich was a North German Protestant, he was, like most of the other Nazi

48

leaders, a Roman Catholic by birth. Hangman Heydrich was born, baptized and brought up a Roman Catholic in Halle. His father, a Protestant, changed his religion when he married Heydrich's well-to-do mother."

Now these facts are clear enough and quite easily believed, especially to Protestants who know Romanism as the cruel and bloody monster that she most certainly is. Much that is stated in Sinclair's book can be verified from other reliable sources, such as **The Secret History Of The Jesuits.**

However, so that we cannot be charged with using one source alone, we will prove the validity of Rivera's claims from additional sources as well.

On pages 240-241 of **The Vatican Against Europe,** we read:

"So far as France was concerned, we have no difficulty in believing that the status of the Jews which was drawn up by the government obtained the Vatican's nihil obstat. In this connection, Leon Poliakov supplies us with an extract of a note from Leon Berard, Ambassador to the Holy See, to Marshal Petain: 'I stated that nothing had ever been said to me at the Vatican that could have been interpreted as a criticism or disapproval on the part of the Holy See of the legislative and regulative acts concerned.' And he adds: 'The proposal for joint action, formulated by the Protestant Church of France at the time of the raids (Jew baiting) in the summer of 1942, was rejected by the dignitaries of the Catholic church.' "

The author then describes how thousands of Jewish children were arrested and sent to the death camps. He concludes that particular section on page 241 with these words:

"This clearly shows that these arrests were subject to the decision of the Vichy government. Now, we have already seen that this government took no decision in the matter without the consent of the Roman Curia. Must we stress the obvious conclusion??"

Pages 238-239 of the above mentioned book will show you that the Nazi campaign into Russia was a modern crusade, set up to convert or punish all heretics, just like the Inquisition.

The conversion of Russia, which Rome had hoped to achieve through the Bolshevik Revolution, was now attempted through the use of a foreign army.

"Count Halke von Ledochowski, Jesuit

General, was disposed to organize, on the common basis of anti-communism, a certain degree of collaboration between the German Secret Service and the Jesuit Order . . .

"Von Ledochowski considered the forthcoming bellicose settling of accounts between Russia and Germany as inevitable . . . And the Baseler Nachrichten (March 27, 1942) did not hesitate to write: 'One of the questions arising from German activity in Russia which is of supreme importance to the Vatican, is the question of the evangelisation of Russia.'

"This is confirmed by Father Duclos himself in a book covered by the Imprimatur – 'During the summer of 1941, Hitler appealed to all Christian forces . . . (he) authorized Catholic missionaries to go to the new eastern territories . . .

"Nor has it been forgotten that, in France, Cardinal Baudrillart and Mgr. Mayol de Luppe recruited the L.V.F. for the crusade against Russia.' "

Charge No. 11:

It is wrong to infer that the Jesuits formed and led the dreaded Ustashi death squads in Yugoslavia.

Answer: Regarding the Romanist persecution of heretics in Yugoslavia, we have so much material it is difficult deciding what to quote and what to leave out.

I will start with the booklet, **Ravening Wolves**, by the late Miss Monica Farrell, a converted Roman Catholic. On the front cover we read:

> "This is the record of torture and murder committed in Europe in 1941-1943 by an army of Catholic Actionists known as the Ustashi, led by monks and priests, and even participated in by nuns. The victims suffered and died in the cause of liberty and freedom of conscience. The least we can do is to read the record of their sufferings and keep in mind that it happened, not in the dark ages, but in our own ENLIGHTENED generation. Ustashi is another name for Catholic Action."

Rather than quote the descriptions of the gruesome massacres, of which the book is full, I will quote evidence against the Roman Institution.

52

"Still further proof is found in the report of seven prominent Protestant clergymen, who travelled from the U.S.A. to Yugoslavia to investigate for themselves and report to their fellow countrymen their findings. These seven investigators were: Dr. G. E. Shipler, editor of **The Churchman**, an Episcopalian. Dr. E. S. Burke, editor of **Zion's Herald**, of Boston, a Methodist. Dr. G. W. Buckner, Jr., editor of **World Call**, of Indianapolis, Disciple of Christ. Dr. P. P. Elliott of the First Presbyterian Church of Brooklyn. Dr. S. Trexler, former President of the Lutheran Synod of New York. Rev. C. Williams, Director of the Institute of Applied Religion, Birmingham, Alabama. Rev. W. H. Melish of the Church of the Holy Trinity, an Episcopalian."

"In their report they say:

"Among the documents we examined were great numbers of official Roman Catholic newspapers and periodicals, frankly telling the story from month to month, of the Archbishop's (that is Stepinac, who was the Primate of the Catholic church in Yugoslavia) collaboration with the Nazi forces. It seemed obvious that the reason for this candid recording of such collaboration was due to the conviction that Germany would win the war. "The documents showed that, when the Ital-

Robert V. Julien
(Ex-Maryknoll missionary)

"As a former priest, I consider Dr. Rivera a precious brother in Christ. His testimony is true and he genuinely loves the Catholic people. He tells them the truth, risking their anger and his life that they might know salvation."

Donna Eubanks
(Ex-Sister Superior)

"I am now a true Christian, by the grace of God, after 23 years as a nun of the Sisters of St. Joseph. I can state, from personal knowledge, that Dr. Rivera is telling the truth about the Roman Catholic system."

Clark Butterfield
(Ex-priest)

"After reading ALBERTO I realized I was not alone in my desire as a former priest to bring salvation to the millions of captives of the Roman Catholic system. I am honored to associate myself with the ministry of Dr. Rivera."

54

ians and Germans swept into Yugoslavia, underground bands of previously organized Roman Catholic laymen, calling themselves 'Crusaders,' and aided by individual priests and militant monks, rose to receive the invaders. . .

"Pavelich and Kuaternik, with the help of their German, Italian and 'Crusader' soldiers, proceeded to carry out the German-sponsored racial program, which advocated the solidifying of a Croatian community by eliminating such minorities as Jews and gypsies, reducing the number of Serbs living in Croatia, and compelling those remaining to turn Roman Catholic.

"Nearly 70,000 of the 80,000 Jews in the entire country were killed or forced to flee, their property being confiscated. 240,000 Serbs became Byzantine Roman Catholics through forced conversions, on pain of death. Those who resisted were shot or stabbed and their bodies thrown into mass graves, which were subsequently found and opened.

"We saw hundreds of sworn depositions attesting to these crimes, made out by relatives or eye-witnesses, and also, in a few cases, by survivors. Serbia Church properties were seized and turned over to Roman Catholic parishes and convents . . . In the total struggle in Yugoslavia 1,700,000 men, women and children perished."

I could easily go on quoting passage after passage from this excellent little book, written by a true saint of God, all of which will confirm exactly what Alberto Rivera and Jack Chick are saying.

We will conclude by referring to the well documented book, **Holocaust In The Independent State Of Croatia**, by Dr. Lazo M. Kostich, published by Liberty – Chicago, 1981:

"In his report dated September 24, 1941, to Ribbentrop's Foreign Ministry in Berlin, Dr. Gerstenmeir related: 'Orthodox circles in Serbia are deeply embittered by Croatian conduct. The Ustashi have forced tens of thousands of Serbs in Croatia to accept the Catholic faith. Those Orthodox who resisted either had their throats cut en-masse (this is to be taken literally) or all their property confiscated and they were expelled, totally destitute.' "

Again on page 18 we read:

"The mass expulsion or forced conversion of the Orthodox to Roman Catholicism was on the agenda. All measures, aiming at the elimination of Serbdom in Croatia were carried out under the slogan enunciated by one of the Croatian ministers: 'We shall massacre the first third of the Serbs, expel the second third from the country and force the final third to accept the Catholic faith, whereupon they will be absorbed by the Catholic element.' Thus, the most official German circles personally present in Croatia at the time admit that:

    a) The massacre of several hundred thousand Serbs occurred:

    b) The official Croatian policy was to effectuate the disappearance of Serbs from Croatia. In a word, "genocide."

Much of the above information is confirmed in two books: **Ustashi Under The Southern Cross**, by M. Jurjevic, published by M. Jurjevic. The second source is the well documented book, **This Is Artukovic**, printed in Australia by Covenanter Press for Protestant Publications.

I will now describe some photographs which are included in the book by Kostich.

* **Page 262:** Three corpses, one of which is a woman murdered by the Catholic Ustashi.

* **Page 263:** The Ustashi carrying the severed head of a Serbian Orthodox priest.

* **Page 264:** Two pictures: (Top) A peasant digs his own grave. Sadistic Ustashi show him the knife with which they will kill him. (Bottom) After the job is done.

* **Page 267:** A Ustashi with a sadistic smile on his face, chopping off a man's head with an axe.

* **Page 267:** The head of the Croatian S.S., the murderer Pavelic, stands in the middle of Croatian Catholic clergy in April, 1942.

* **Page 277:** The leader of the Ustashi, Pavelic, among Croatian Franciscan monks.

* **Page 278:** The Franciscan, Filipovic, as a priest and in the other picture, in Ustashi uniform, as Commandant of the concentration camp of Jasenovac.

Now we will describe some pictures from **The Vatican Against Europe.** On pages 224 and 225 there are some pictures showing:

1. A family meeting of the Pontifical Legate,

Marcone in the house of Pavelic, the murderer.

2. Archbishop Stepinac and the Pontifical Legate, Marcone, attending a Military parade in Zagreb, surrounded by Italian, German and Ustashi officers.

3. Roman Catholic clergy "blessing" the swastika flag.

Charge No. 12:

It's false to say that Jesuits: 1.) Prepared Fifth Columns in Allied (non-Axis) nations, and, 2.) Prepared secret commando cells in the U.S.A.

Answer: Avro Manhattan's **The Vatican Moscow Washington Alliance,** says on page 265:

"To talk about Catholic fifth columnists sounds discriminatory. Yet, one generation ago, Catholic minorities helped to destroy democratic Europe. This they did by cooperating with Hitler."

On page 266 of the same book we read:

"Again, who were gathered inside the
Trojan Horses to help Hitler topple the
political and, yes, even the military
structures of Belgium and France? Once
more we find individual Catholic leaders or Catholic groups intimately connected with the hierarchies and therefore, with the Vatican and Pope Pius XII
. . . In France, we meet a Papal knight,
Pierre Laval; a Jesuit trained general,
Weygand; and another prominent
Catholic, Marshal Petain. . . . If active
Catholic minorities contributed to the
disintegration of European democracy,
an active Catholic minority could do the
same in the United States."

For confirmation of the above, see pages 140-
141 of **The Vatican Against Europe**. For secret
Jesuit "commando cells" in the U.S.A., see page
139 of **The Secret History Of The Jesuits.**

Again, the claims of Rivera and Chick are proven
to be true. Thank God for those who have the
courage to let the truth be known about this great
enemy of freedom and Christian righteousness
– the Roman Catholic church.

The Tactic

Most of the charges against Alberto Rivera have
been direct attacks against the integrity and

Official Certification

This is a copy of the last official certification that was given to Alberto Rivera just before he left Spain in 1967. He received copies in both Spanish and English.

ARZOBISPADO
DE
MADRID-ALCALA
CANCILLERIA SECRETARIA

Su Excelencia Reverendísima, el Señor
Obispo Auxiliar y Vicario General de esta
Arzobispado, ha tenido a bien autorizar a
D. Alberto Rivera
Romero
Sacerdote que reside en esta Archidiócesis,
para que pueda salir al extranjero por
motivos de su ministerio

Madrid, 14 de septiembre de 196 7

EL CANCILLER SECRETARIO.

M. Cano

SPANISH

ARCHBISHOPRIC
OF
MADRID-ALCALA
CHANCELLERY-SECRETARYSHIP

His Most Reverend Excellency the Auxi-
liary Bishop and Vicar-General of this
Archbishopric is pleased to authorize
Mr. Alberto Rivera Romero, a priest that
dwells in this Archdiocese, to go into
foreign countries in the cause of his
ministry . . . .

Madrid, September 14, 1967

Chancellery-Secretary

Seal Of The Secretary
Of The Archbishopric Of
Madrid-Alcala-Spain.
State of Tennessee |
Bradley County |
    I, Daniel G. Ahrego, make oath in due form of law that the
furegoing is a true and correct translation of the instrument attached
here to.

sworn to and subscribed before me   Daniel H. Ahrego
this 20th day of April, 1968
                    Notary Public State at large

ENGLISH

61

validity of his claim that he was a Roman Catholic Jesuit and that his experiences were genuine. This approach is better described as character assassination. It is usually used in desperation by people who cannot honestly refute the facts.

Those who use this approach to criticize Dr. Rivera usually begin their string of lies with statements like, "Detailed research has shown that . . ." On occasions, they try to add validity to their claims by pulling quotes from compromising ecumenical "Christian" publications that do not want to offend the Roman Catholic church.

The fact that Rome has resorted to vicious and unrelenting character assassination attempts against Alberto Rivera is some of the surest proof that the claims he has made about Rome are right on the money. If his claims were false, the Catholic hierarchy would have proven him wrong years ago and he would surely have faded like the setting sun. So you see, the Roman church itself, by its very actions, proves that Rivera is telling the truth.

The religious crowd in Jesus' day hated Him because He exposed their sin. Today's religious crowd will despise you as well if you begin shining light on their sinful ways. Alberto Rivera is living proof. Consider this portion of scripture:

"For every one that doeth evil hateth the

light, neither cometh to the light, lest his deeds should be reproved (examined)."   John 3:20

No wonder there has been such a vicious propaganda campaign against Dr. Rivera. Who has shone more light on Rome's wicked darkness than this one man?

Who's Doing The Lying?

It is very interesting that the Catholic church would accuse Dr. Rivera of lying, for when it comes to telling outright falsehoods, Rome leads the field. How much trust can we put in Rome's denials of Rivera? Not one bit, especially in view of the following, which comes from Lesson 17 – "The Love and Service of Man" from **The Catholic Religion** published by The Catholic Enquiry Centre, Maroubra, N.S.W. 1979. It says:

> "It is lawful sometimes to conceal the truth or part of it. There are occasions when it would be harmful to oneself or others to tell the whole truth. It is not sinful to make ambiguous statements or make mental reservations on certain issues as when a person is bound by secrecy, or is questioned by one who has no right to certain information."

So Rome says it's permissible for them to lie when

it best serves their purposes, yet they condemn Rivera for being a liar. Besides being hypocritical, their position makes a mockery of scripture:

" . . . **all liars**, shall have their part in the lake which burneth with fire and brimstone: which is the second death."
Revelation 21: 8

"**Lying lips** are an abomination to the Lord: but they that deal truly are his delight."   Proverbs 12: 22

"These six things doth the Lord **hate**; yea, seven are an abomination unto him: a proud look, **a lying tongue**, and hands that shed innocent blood,"
Proverbs 6: 16,17

In light of Rome's statement about lying, I ask again – how much can we trust their claims about Rivera? Very simple. Not one bit.

Proof that the Catholic church does indeed believe that it is permissible to "conceal the truth" can be found in their numerous false and unbiblical doctrines. Here are just a few:

1. That Mary is a Mediatrix between God and men ... a lie. (I Timothy 2:5)

2. That Mary, the mother of Jesus, was im-

maculately conceived... a lie.
(Romans 3:23)

3. That the priest can forgive sins...a lie.
(I John 1:9)

4. That Peter was the first Pope...a lie.
(Acts 10:25,26)

5. That the Pope is infallible...a lie.
(Romans 3:23)

6. That money paid into its coffers can help
souls after death...a lie. (Hebrews 9:27)

7. That salvation is to be found in her alone...
a lie. (John 14:6)

8. That priests can turn a biscuit into the
living Christ...a lie. (Hebrews 10:10, 12)

9. That idol worship (i. e. crucifixes, rosary
beads, statues, saints, etc.) is right...a lie.
(Exodus 20:4-5)

10. That "holy water" can perform miracles...
a lie. (e.g., STATE AFFAIR item – Jan.,
1986)

11. That the Catholic church is poor...a lie.
(Read **The Vatican Billions,** by Avro
Manhattan.)

12. That she saved thousands of Jews in Rome during Nazi occupation....a lie. (Read the truth on page 29 of the book **The Vatican Papers.**)

Now, after considering these few Rome-inspired lies (many more could be given), can any person with a sound mind give a scrap of credence to anything this evil system might say about men like Alberto Rivera? Of course not!

In fact, we would go so far as to say that if Rome agreed with Rivera in all that he says, then we would be highly skeptical of the man ourselves. Rome's denunciations of him only further establish the truth of what he says.

Was he a Jesuit?

Proof of the fact that Rivera was in fact a Jesuit can be found through several items, including:

* His Spanish Identity Card.

* A letter of authorization by the Archbishop of Madrid – Alcala.

* Pictures showing him in priestly garb in a parish school.

With proof like this, the Catholic church cannot simply dismiss it all and say that he never really belonged to their system. The proof is available for all to examine – proof as good as any man can possibly produce.

It is interesting to note that ex-Romanists like former Maryknoll missionary Robert V. Julien, former Sister Superior Donna Eubanks and former priest Clark Butterfield all agree that according to their extensive experiences in the Catholic church, Rivera's claims are true.

Another interesting fact is that many ex-Roman Catholics who are truly saved by the grace of God have no problem in agreeing with Rivera's claims. They know what the Roman Catholic system is like from personal experience.

It seems that those Christians who believe the lies Rome is circulating about Rivera have been made drunk with the wine of her fornication and cannot discern between truth and falsehood.

Of course, Rome will deny Rivera's exposure of her evil system. Did she not trump up false charges against Chiniquy when he exposed her? Read **Fifty Years In The "Church" Of Rome** and let that truth grip your heart.

What about the famous Dreyfus Affair, which divided France before the turn of the last century? False documents were provided to condemn an innocent military officer to life in prison. According to Edmond Paris in chapter 8 of his book, **The Secret History Of The Jesuits**, it was the Roman institution which was behind the whole sickly affair. The Bible tells us to expect such a reaction from those who are servants of darkness. When Jesus exposed the false religious system of His day, He was crucified.

It must not be forgotten that "holy mother church" claims never to change. As far as her campaign of lies and deception is concerned, we fully agree with her. She has never changed her lying ways.

From the reading of good sound Protestant books, we soon learn that Rome's history is pregnant with examples of the use of character assassination to destroy her enemies when all else has failed to discredit them.

Could Protestants Justify Killing?

Could true blood-washed Protestants, either of to-day or of the past, commit the same heinous crimes the Catholic church has, and not be exposed? Examine the history of the Protestants:

1. Which of the great Protestant Reformers was guilty of the torture and murder of tens of thousands of innocent people in the past?

2. Have men like Huss, Luther, Calvin, Knox, Cranmer, Ridley, Latimer, or more recently,

Wesley or Whitefield, a record of torture and murder to their credit? Where or when did these men boldly proclaim that the church has the right to kill those who disagree with them?

3. In which Protestant church's articles of faith will you find a provision made to exterminate those of different persuasion?

We must not confuse, for example, the execution of Romanists who took part in the Gunpowder Plot, and who were subsequently punished by King James for their crimes.

We must not confuse examples like this with the extermination of so-called heretics by the Roman Institution. Romanists were executed for crimes against legal government; Protestants were put to death for their faith in God and His Word. Those are two very different sets of circumstances.

Let us never forget:

> * The Reformers cried out against this
>   evil system.

> * Those who have recently left the
>   Roman fold agree with what Alberto
>   says.

Where are today's genuine blood-washed Protestants? Thousands who have been redeemed by the blood of Christ should be standing faithfully beside Rivera and Chick in their efforts to expose this anti-christ religious system.

It must never be forgotten that as a denomination, Rome claims that she is the one and only true church. She contends that the Catholic church was set up by Christ who left as His successor, Peter, the Pope and universal head. She claims that outside of her, there is **no** salvation. This is cultism in its most arrogant and devilish form.

What a sad state of affairs we have reached when supposed Bible believing Christian people will side with a lying anti-christ system like this against a man who is endeavoring to expose her false teachings.

TESTIMONIES

My Catholic neighbors researched the truth in ALBERTO and DOUBLE-CROSS from their own church library. They left their church, announcing to us, "We are no longer Catholics."　　Albany, GA

• • • • • • •

I sent my brother ALBERTO and DOUBLE-CROSS. He was pulled one way and back another for a couple of weeks and finally, following the steps in the back of the comics. acknowledged his sin and asked Christ to save him. Like myself, he was a Roman Catholic, but now is a Child of God.　　Robbinsville, NC

• • • • • • •

I had two friends who read ALBERTO; one of them was outraged, but now both of them are saved and attending a Bible believing church. Both of them were Roman Catholics.　　Rock Hill, SC

• • • • • • •

My brother boldly took my mother (a strict Catholic) a copy of ALBERTO, for which I got after him. I felt that it would anger and alienate her. IT LED HER TO CALVARY! She is now in His service, has read her Bible from cover to cover in less than four weeks, and is witnessing to all of her friends. Laredo, TX

Chapter 2

Private Investigation of Alberto

Following are the six titles in a series of Crusaders comic books published by Chick Publications, which are based on information that was submitted by ex-Jesuit priest, Alberto Rivera:

As a result of the numerous accusations that were made against the Catholic church in these comics, the supposed Christian periodical, **Christianity Today**, unleashed a scathing character assassination of Alberto Rivera. Since they could not refute the facts he presented, they did the only thing they could; discredit his testimony by attacking him personally.

To determine if the charges against Dr. Rivera that were printed in **Christianity Today** were valid or not, the Canadian Protestant League (which is not affiliated with Alberto Rivera or Jack Chick in any way) conducted their own investigation of these accusations. They printed their findings in the September, 1983 issue of its official organ, **The Protestant Challenge.**

We have reproduced a portion of that report here to further substantiate the fact that Alberto Rivera is in fact for real:

"Booklets produced in comic form by Chick Publications in cooperation with Dr. Alberto M. R. Rivera (viz.: ALBERTO, DOUBLE-CROSS, THE GODFATHERS, SABOTAGE, THE BIG BETRAYAL, and more recently, THE FORCE) have excited angry responses from the Roman Catholic hierarchy across this continent. The said publications have been called hate propaganda, and demands have been made that they be banned. These are familiar demands, used for generations against those who have dared to expose and oppose the false claims, doctrines and practices of Roman Catholicism.

"The books have been described by papal representatives (as well as by those duped by Jesuit propaganda) as 'absurd, bigoted, a comedy of errors, condemning out of hatred, dangerous to the cause of Christ, disgusting, distortion of truth, evil spirit inspired, false, filthy, hatred, hogwash, lewd, lies, malicious, playing fast and loose with truth, Satan possessed, shameful, spiritual pornography, trash, stupidity, ugly,' as well as 'working for the Devil and not Jesus, immoral and indecent!'

"Christian bookstores have been coaxed, awed and threatened into discontinuing sales of the Crusaders series, and every other piece of material published by Chick – even its Gospel tracts.

"At the head office of the Canadian Protestant League, we have attracted a little more than our share of attention, innuendo and threat by legal and other means. (We only started to handle the material when we became aware of the aggressive campaign to remove it from the scene.) Two of the books were banned from entry into Canada on instructions by a Director of Canada Customs and Excise on the grounds of 'immorality and indecency.' We challenged that outra-

74

geous action in Court and the order was re-
scinded.

"Efforts have been made in other areas to deny
the use of the Post Offices to those who continued to send the material through the mails. We
were warned that a report to the R.C.M.P. was
being made against us.

"We are threatened by the appointment of a
study committee, responsible to the Attorney-
General of Ontario, at the urging of the office of
the R.C. Archbishop of Toronto, to determine
whether ALBERTO and DOUBLE-CROSS
should be designated as 'Hate Literature,' and
appropriate charges laid. We have been visited
by two inspectors of Metropolitan Toronto Police, enquiring about our involvement, and
speaking of the possibility of action against us.

"We made no effort to hide any of our activity,
but admitted freely that we were selling the
items they were asking about. We repeated to
them what we had told others: we would wel-
come a charge being laid against us under the
Hate Propaganda Section of Canada's criminal
code.

"We believe that when any pressure group can
successfully intimidate all Christian booksellers
across Canada into refraining to sell certain

literature because it is OFFENSIVE to some, then surely someone ought to be ready to focus attention on such a threat to faith and freedom in this land of ours.

"We are prepared to take that action.

"We have been reminded of the possibility of a $6,000.00 fine or a two-year prison sentence. We have insisted, if and when this should take place, that no one will pay the fine! Perhaps this will arouse apathetic Canadians – and apathetic Christians.

"One would expect Roman Catholics (feeling their own institutions were assailed) to rally every effort to offset the most effective, fruitful harvest the said literature is able to report, but the more tragic form of attack from those who glory in the label of 'evangelical Christians' makes sad reading indeed!

"**Christian Reader**, **Cornerstone** and **Our Sunday Visitor**, published an article authored by Gary Metz entitled, 'The Uncomical Alberto Rivera,' a prominent article in **Christianity Today**.

"More recently, an effort by Brian Onken in **Forward**, the official organ of Christian Research Institute, appeared under the title, 'Alberto: The

Truth About His Story.' In this 'study,' Dr. Rivera, the converted Jesuit priest, is represented as being a dishonest fraud. Areas are named in the United States wherein Alberto was allegedly being sought for questioning.

"The articles demand a response from those who are jealous in contending for the faith and to conserve our freedom. Concerned Christians wish to hear answers to several questions:

"Is Jack Chick a totally irresponsible publisher?

"Is Alberto Rivera the lying sensationalist he is caricatured as being?

"Is Alberto truly God's instrument for our day to bring about the longed-for reawakening among duped Roman Catholics, so that they can be truly won to Jesus Christ as Lord, Saviour, Mediator and Advocate; to the Bible as the Word of God, authoritative, free from error, inspired, and reliable to judge all other authorities; and directing people to come out of an organization that is anti-Christian?

"Why the terrible abuse and attack upon these two brethren?

"Why has someone not followed up on some of the charges made? Can we not analyze the charges? Can we not forensically analyze the charges made?

'Will the men and magazines, hailed by many as authoritative in the field of evangelism, allow us to examine their charges? We want to know if they have a case at all!

"If their charges can be logically and evidentially supported, so that we must see Dr. Rivera as guilty beyond a reasonable doubt, then we must re-examine our own position and alter our stance of supporting Chick and Rivera.

"Now – what is contained in the expose, coming to us in these articles? Alas, they are being accepted by those who have never taken the trouble to thoughtfully and thoroughly investigate the charges against the brethren.

"Are these criticisms dependent upon hearsay evidence, rumour, reported information, charges of fraud, usually reliable sources, deception, controversy, disturbance, questioned reliability, untruths, continual lying, defiance, contradictory testimony and ingenuity in attempts to validate his own story? This is the sort of language of those who sit in judgment upon Dr. Rivera.

"Can it be that the wish is the parent of the

thought? Do these accusers want the stories to be true? These are the questions calling for definitely stated answers; and that is what we are seeking.

Examine The Charges!

"These magazines – upon which so many people rely – make statements concerning Dr. Rivera with no presentation of supportive evidence. This is so obvious, it is difficult to assess the writings accusing the man.

"Now, imagine we are sitting in a Court of Law and serious charges are laid against Alberto Rivera. The Prosecution does its utmost presenting its charges and its testimony supporting those charges.

"The Defence Attorney, if he considers that evidence weak, will move that no case has been established, and ask the Magistrate to dismiss the charges. Should the Judge agree, the Accused is released. He is assumed to be innocent!

"We want to observe the charges, and consider how well those making the charges substantiate them. Should they not be properly supported in the presentations, then we ask that they be dismissed, and that apologies be made to the brethren charged. The Bible tells us as Christians:

'Do violence to no man, neither accuse any falsely. Prove all things, hold fast that which is good. Against an elder receive not an accusation, but before two or three witnesses. In the mouth of two or three witnesses shall every word be established.'

"Did the critics read Alberto's outline of the Basic Steps followed by the Roman Hierarchy to discredit and destroy any who left their ranks? Did they endeavour to expose Romanism's errors and evil practices? Did they insist that Jesuitism is not, by any means Christian?

"In his defence against what he describes as slanders levelled by friend and foe alike, Rivera calls attention to . . . unchristian and anti-biblical charges and accusations by the head of the Christian Research Center (which carefully avoids research into the crimes and massacres of the Roman Catholic institution) through the instrumentality of articles appearing in . . . **Cornerstone** and **Christianity Today** . . .

"An honest, decent person, even a non-Christian, will recognize the validity and credibility of Dr. Rivera as a Roman Catholic priest! Why have these critics consistently attacked Alberto Rivera instead of the doctrines he espouses and proclaims?

"Mr. Metz says: Alberto says he worked with notable Jesuit spies such as Kathryn Kuhlman and Jim Jones; yet nowhere and at no time has Rivera said he had worked with either one!

> *"Indeed, enquiries have been made by the Canadian Protestant League of every one of the police jurisdictions mentioned by the accusers, and consistently the response has been, we have never heard of this man!"*

"The critics tell us that the story of Alberto was banned by the Christian Reformed Church, Zondervan Publishers and The Southern Baptist Sunday School Board; yet failed to admit that many of the congregations associated with these three bodies continue to sell the Crusaders Comics in question.

"The critics failed to ask the Roman Catholic hierarchy why they were upset because the articles were true, for because of them thousands of former Roman Catholics had found Jesus Christ as Lord and Saviour, and were coming out of Rome's religion.

"Why else should a priest on an Indian Reservation in New Brunswick order a faith missionary to stay off the Reserve, if it were not that many young native adults were reading of Alberto through the comics and were coming to Christ? This has been true in Western Canada and in some places in Ontario.

"Why did not the critics ask the representatives of the Roman Church why these demands they currently make to ban from entry, etc., unless it is for fear of an acceleration of many of their people in this exodus from Rome?

"Why, specifically, are the mentioned publishers trying to abolish the ALBERTO series from all of their outlets? Have they been asked? Have they been asked whether the local Roman Church representatives have not appealed for this because they are offensive to them? (This was the reason given by the office of the Toronto

R.C. Archbishop.) We are told by the critics: Our investigation reveals (Rivera's) police record, his investment schemes, his bad cheque-writing, his contradictory testimony, his fabricated education record, and his reported family abuse. Yet the author of these words must have forgotten something! He neglected to quote from any court records (indeed does not mention any single Court record location, any dates, any case numbers, and charges filed, whether or not an arrest was made, and the final outcome of the levelled charges allegedly made).

"Reported abuse, newspaper clippings, magazine articles, several article writers (each quoting the others), never must be understood to be valid, factual evidence credible of anything at all! Critical mention is made of a college in Spain for which Rivera (as a Jesuit priest) was authorized to collect funds, when he was not properly authorized to do so.

"The articles claim that Rivera was never a priest. No mention is made of the name of the college, or the source of the information to support the conclusions. It was officially agreed from Roman Catholic sources that Dr. Rivera had indeed been appointed to act in the collection of funds for one month, and surely he would have not been so used without his priestly credentials being checked!

"We are told that a minister of The Church of God of Prophecy, had experienced embarrassment when Rivera allegedly had written a cheque on an already closed account.

"Yet no mention is made of the location of the minister, of the banks concerned, of the locality of the airline desk complaining, whether the writers had ever seen a copy of the cheque, whether the closed account had previously existed, or to which office of which Department the said minister had written a complaint. (True, the accusers give us the name of the minister, but nothing else.)

"Charges are made of a history of legal entanglements, court actions, accusations of fraud, warrants issued for arrest, writing of bad cheques; yet no specifics regarding complaints, vital details, police records, places, hearings. No results are reported at all.

"Indeed, enquiries have been made by the Canadian Protestant League of every one of the police jurisdictions mentioned by the accusers, and consistently the response has been, we have never heard of this man!

"We hear of alleged inconsistencies, contradictions, impossibly conflicting dates; yet we have never been given the sources of such information

84

– letters, tapes, photo-copies, individuals, interviews, etc. – not even a newspaper clipping!

"We are told: Alberto's claim to have been a Jesuit priest and bishop is denied by Roman Catholic spokesmen. They state the documents he exhibits as proof of this priesthood are little more than form letters giving permission to travel abroad.

"What else would one expect? Surely we would not expect Roman Catholic officialdom to admit that Alberto Rivera is telling the truth about them or their Jesuitical practices! How naive are we expected to be?"

This thorough and honest report, which was produced by a source completely separate from both Alberto and Chick, strips away the facade and reveals the facts behind the smokescreen.

Alberto Rivera is exactly what he says he is, a former Jesuit priest who was converted to Christ. The vicious character assassination attempts made against him only go to prove the veracity of his statements about Rome.

Chapter 3

Answer To Article In Christianity Today

Christianity Today is the title of a very ecumenical magazine. Though it is supposedly a Christian periodical, true Bible-believing Christians were not surprised when **Christianity Today** attacked Alberto Rivera and the information he has presented.

Three pages of their March 13, 1981 issue were devoted to "proving Alberto to be a fraud."

Did the magazine honestly believe Alberto to be a fraud or was there another reason for their actions? Many interesting questions are raised:

* Did they attack Alberto for fear of angering their Roman Catholic readers and los-

ing money through falling subscriptions?

* Is it possible that the Catholics are really in control of the magazine and that they organized the whole smear campaign to discredit Alberto in the eyes of those who believe **Christianity Today** is really a Christian magazine?

* Is **Christianity Today** even Christian to begin with?

As a result of the magazine article, a former Roman Catholic named James M. Houston wrote a letter to **Christianity Today** in answer to their attacking article about Rivera.

We reprint part of his letter as further proof of the validity of what Alberto Rivera has said. Please keep in mind that James Houston is in no way connected to either Alberto Rivera or Jack Chick.

Part of his letter reads as follows:

"I have read your three page article exposing J. T. Chick's 'Alberto' to be a fraud (see Christianity Today, March 13, 1981). I would like to make the following comments on the same hoping that God in His sovereignty would allow this letter to be printed (in full) in a future issue of Christianity Today:

1. Considering the evidence set forth in your article, though I find many things stated of which Alberto Rivera may or may not be guilty, I can find no evidence in the article that proves him to be a fraud, unless of course, I'm misunderstanding the word: 'fraud.' You do state what Rome herself has to say about Alberto. Who in a right frame of mind (unless they are totally ignorant of history) would give heed to her words in the light of the following evidence:

a.) Her teaching that 'the end justifies the means' allows her the freedom to lie, just as long as it propagates her cause.

b.) H. G. Wells, noted historian, in his book, **Crux Ansata**, states:

Page 105 – 'Roman Catholicism is a broken and utterly desperate thing, capable only of malignant mischief in our awakening world.'

Page 155 – 'I think that it stands for everything most hostile to the mental emancipation and stimulation of mankind. It is the completest, most highly organized system of prejudices and antagonisms in existence. Everywhere in the world there is ignorance and prejudice, but the greatest complex of these, with the most extensive prestige and the most intimate entanglement with traditional institutions, is the Roman Catholic Church. It presents many faces towards the world, but everywhere it is systematic in its fight against freedom.'

c.) Lord Macaulay, says on page 548 of his 1852 **Essays On Ranke's History Of The Popes**:

It is impossible to deny that the polity of the Church of Rome is the very masterpiece of human wisdom. . . . The experience of 1,200 eventful years, the ingenuity and patient care of forty generations of statesmen, have improved that polity to such perfection, that, among the contrivances which have been devised **for deceiving and controlling mankind, it occupies the highest place.'**

"But even with such a great cloud of witnesses, one might be tempted to ask the following question, 'Has not Rome changed recently?' To answer this most vital question, I turn once again to the message of D. Martyn Lloyd Jones:

'Ah, but,' you say, 'has not the Roman Catholic Church changed? You are simply looking back, you are speaking as if you lived in the 16th century – don't you realize you are living in the 20th century?

My answer is quite simple. The proudest boast of the Roman Catholic Church is this, that she never changes, Semper eadem. How can she change? If she changes she will be admitting that she was wrong in the past – but she was saying then that she was infallible, and that the Pope is the Vicar of Christ and that he cannot make a mistake. If she says that she is capable of change she is denying her central claim! She does not say that she is changing, and she never will. The Church of Rome remains the same.

If anything, she is even worse. She has 'added' things to what she taught in the 16th century, such as Papal infallibility, etc. No, there is no change in the Church of Rome. And if there ever is one great world

Church, it will be because the Church of Rome has absorbed all the rest and swallowed them in ignorance!'

"In the light of all this evidence, should we give any logical credence to what Rome has to say about the persons of Jack Chick and Alberto Rivera? God forbid!

"Secondly, getting back to Alberto Rivera and your accusation against him and the Chick organization, I do not believe that Jack Chick would jeopardize his well-grounded ministry without some definite leading of the Holy Spirit. Surely he would never put himself in such jeopardy unless he was quite sure Alberto was genuine.

"Just a small consideration of what Rome has done to those who exposed her in the past tells me that Chick has laid his very life on the line. And what of his dear family? Has he not also jeopardized them?

"Thirdly, I must consider Alberto himself. Why would he also put himself and his dear family in such jeopardy? What could he possibly gain by such a move? No, logic moves me to conclude that he is being led by the Holy Spirit of our dear Lord. God bless his brave heart!

"Fourthly, I must consider Satan's part in all this, in the light of what Jesus says in Matthew 12:25-26:

"I have never read anything against J. T. Chick until he attacked Rome."

'Every kingdom divided against itself is brought to desolation . . . And if Satan cast out Satan, he is divided against himself; how shall his kingdom stand?'

"In the light of the much proven fact that Rome has always been a devilish system and the curse of everything it touches, I doubt very seriously that the Devil himself would author a book that at least has started people once again thinking about the great evil of Rome. The Devil may not be wise, but he is shrewd and cunning.

"Fifthly, I must also consider the true, holy, living Christians that I personally know. And though they be few, yet they are in agreement that this is of God.

"Sixthly, though Rome has proven herself to be the greatest fraud ever put off on mankind, I do not recall your magazine going to any great length to expose her as such, even though such a move on your part would be a most blessed benefit to all of mankind, especially the body of Christ.

"Again, I must ask the question, why is your magazine so anxious to expose dear Alberto? A good question, for even if I thought for a moment that this book, ALBERTO, was set forth in pretense, could not my heart rejoice (as the Apostle Paul does in Philippians 1:18) that once again this 'mother of all spiritual whoredoms' is being brought again to the attention of the TRUE sheep of God? I must say that I am very suspicious of your motive in printing this article.

"Also, I noted on the second page of your article where the Roman Catholic Editor of **Our Sunday Visitor** states: '...The sad thing is that Chick's lies are hard to refute.' It may be that they are 'hard to refute' simply because they are true! Amen!

"And last, I must consider the fact that to my remembrance (and I read extensively) **I have never read anything against J. T. Chick UNTIL he attacked Rome.** The Devil's mad and I'm so glad! Hallelujah!

"I could go on, but I'm afraid I may have labored you too much already, so I will stop. I do pray that this letter will be received in the spirit in which it is written; and God willing, may the truth set forth in it reach the hearts of many DEAR souls, lest they end up with the mark of the Beast. May God also encourage your heart to search this matter out diligently, lest you be found to be fighting against the very Spirit of Truth, Himself, even our dear Lord.

"Written by one who loves Jesus and hates the DEVOUT enemies of Jesus with that PERFECT hatred that David speaks of in Psalm 139:21-22, I remain,

Someone who is praying for you,
(signed) James M. Houston"

In this letter, Mr. Houston asks some very good questions. For example:

1. Why is Christianity Today so anxious to condemn a man who is exposing a false religious system?

2. Where's the proof to substantiate the allegations that are leveled against Alberto? The article is long on accusations, but solid proof is conspicuously absent.

3. **Christianity Today** says the Catholic church denies that Alberto was ever a priest. Would you expect them to come out and admit that he was? Never!

While the article was designed to discredit and smear Alberto, a careful reading of it only reinforces the information this servant of God has presented.

Conclusion

In light of all this, how can any honest person believe the Roman-inspired lies about A. Rivera and J. Chick? We have presented independent evidence which heavily supports Rivera's charges against the Roman church, evidence which can be obtained by anyone without much difficulty.

We offer this challenge to any so-called "expert on the cults," or any other skeptic. Before you accuse these two fine Christian brethren, first get your facts right. Attacking the cults is good and useful; however, don't focus on the minor cults without exposing the biggest, most evil and dangerous one first. Otherwise, don't be surprised if true born-again Bible-believing Christians view your efforts with suspicion.

Before you accuse either of them of "hating Catholics," find out what you're talking about. It is not hate, but true love, that motivates these men to cry out to deceived lost souls perishing in a false religion. Who is guilty of hate? Men who try to awaken and rescue the perishing, or pious religious leaders who deceive multitudes and help push them into the eternal flames of hell?

No, it is neither Rivera or Chick who are guilty of hate. They are to be commended for their genuine love and compassion for the lost. If you care to discuss hate, study the history of the Catholic institution. Their past is replete with acts that perfectly define the word hate.